CALLED TO KNIGHTHOOD:

The Sacrament of Confirmation in the Kingdom Family of God

THOMAS K. SULLIVAN

CALLED TO KNIGHTHOOD:

The Sacrament of Confirmation
in the Kingdom Family of God

THOMAS K. SULLIVAN

SIMON PETER PRESS

Simon Peter Press, Inc.

PO Box 2187

Oldsmar, FL 34677

ISBN: 0-9777430-8-X

978-0-9777430-8-7

Cover and Interior design by Jacinta Calcut, Image Graphics & Design

PRINTED IN THE UNITED STATES OF AMERICA

DEDICATION

This book is dedicated to my father and mother, Thomas Andrew and Pauline Sophia Sullivan. To my father, for always demonstrating the true character of a man and teaching me by his example what it means to be a godly man, a loving husband and a strong father. To my mother, for her unwavering love, patience, faith and endless hours she spent on her knees in prayer for me throughout the course of my life, especially in the most difficult of times. It is with the deepest of love and devotion I dedicate this book to them.

TABLE OF CONTENTS

PART I

PREFACE

The following study of the Sacrament of Confirmation is the result of much research into the Church's continued teaching on the Sacrament over the past 2000 years, as well as my experience as a Confirmation Coordinator at St. Cyprian Parish in the Archdiocese of Los Angeles. It is in no way an exhaustive explanation nor is it a complex theological thesis. It is simply a summary of the many hundreds of hours of research and study on my own journey to discover the meaning of the Sacrament of Confirmation. It is written in laymen's terms for the understanding of lay people.

I think it is true to say that the Sacrament of Confirmation is probably the least understood and most underrated sacrament of them all. For this reason, I will begin our investigation by first looking at the Biblical framework of the family of God and then, with this as background, review the Church's teaching on the meaning of Confirmation, the strict obligation that comes with Confirmation, and the indescribable gift that God bestows on the one confirmed.

From there I will attempt to deal with current misconceptions about the Sacrament of Confirmation; what it IS and, what it IS NOT; the current confusion over the age of Confirmation; and finally, some practical suggestions for the restructuring of many of the religious education programs in our country.

INTRODUCTION

The magnitude of the Sacrament of Confirmation can be grasped somewhat when one looks at what the Sacred Congregation for Divine Worship stated in its 1971 Rite of Confirmation:

"One of the highest responsibilities of the people of God is to prepare the baptized for Confirmation." (DOL. 2512)

What is it about the Sacrament of Confirmation that puts such a high degree of responsibility on the people of God to prepare the baptized for this sacrament? This question and others will be answered as we go on.

The Sacrament of Confirmation has been known by many different names over the centuries:

A. Mystical Chrism. (St. Cyril of Jerusalem, 350 A.D.)
B. Sanctification by Chrism.
    (Pope St. Leo the Great, 440-461 A.D.)
C. Laying on of the Hands. (Innocent III, 1198-1216)
D. The Anointing of the Forehead with Chrism.
    (Innocent IV, 1243-1254)
E. The Holy Chrism of Confirmation.
    (Council of Trent, 1545-1563)
F. Rite of Confirmation.
    (Vatican Council II, 1962-1965)
G. Rite of Chrismation. (Eastern Rite Churches)
H. Sacrament of Christian Maturity. (Modern Times)

Regardless of what name the sacrament has been called, the official teaching of the Church has never changed in terms of what the sacrament confers upon the baptized. Now there are many aspects to Confirmation, all of which result from this sacrament. But the primary aspect from which all the others originate is the fact that Confirmation strenthens us as *"Soldiers of Christ"* and *"strictly obligates us to spread and defend the faith by both word and deed."* (See Biblical Origins and Implicit References at the end of Part One for support of this statement.)

In order to better understand what Confirmation really is, we must first understand who, and what, the family of God is. But this understanding cannot be in 21st Century (modern day), social structural terms. We must understand the family of God in the terms that God chose to use when He identified Himself as our Father and we became His children. Therefore, to begin this, we must refer to the written Word of God, Sacred Scripture, and see just how God fathered His chosen family, Israel, and see how its "family structure" was organized.

Old Testament Background

The King: If we were high above the earth looking down on the history of the Old and New Testaments, we would have a beautiful bird's eye view of how God structured His family. One of the first things we would notice is that God's chosen nation, Israel, has a king (or ruler). (Deut 17:14-17; 1 Sam 8:1-9) Israel did not have a president or any other official elected by the people, as we do in this country. A king assumes the throne he inherits from his father. This is known as dynastic succession. Initially, God established His kingdom under the kingship of David; and, we refer to it now as the Davidic Dynasty. The next thing we notice is that Israel is not only a nation but also a kingdom—a kingdom of priests, prophets and kings. A kingdom is different from our society because it is a monarchical form of government, meaning, that the solemn rule of authority rests in one person—a king or a queen.

The Queen Mother: The next point that must be made is that every king who reigned over Israel, beginning with King Solomon, had his mother seated next to him on the throne (1 Kings 2:19; 2 Kings 12:1; 14:2; 15:2). She was known as the Queen Mother, and was considered the mother to all of Israel and to all those in the kingdom as long as her son was on the throne.

Structure and Cabinet Members: A kingdom is also hierarchical in structure with various offices established, and men were appointed by the king to fill these offices. They were not voted in by the people as we do in this country (2 Sam 8:15; 1 Kings 4; Isaiah 22:19-22).

Warriors/Knights of the Kingdom: Another aspect of a kingdom is that it has warriors, or soldiers that defend and spread the kingdom (1 Sam 17; 2 Sam 8; 2 Sam 18). A kingdom is helpless without soldiers to protect the king, the queen mother, and the members of that kingdom from being attacked. The soldiers of a kingdom play a crucial role in the survival of the kingdom. In our country, we only read about these soldiers in our literature and history books and know them as "knights in shining armor." We recall some of these knights: King Arthur, Sir Lancelot and the Knights of the Round Table, Sir Galahad, Joan of Arc, and many others. The term "knight" also has another meaning as well as that of "soldier," and that is *one who is devoted to the service of a lady as her attendant or champion.* (Webster's Collegiate Dictionary)

Now you might be wondering what all of this has to do with Confirmation. Well, first we must look at all the facts. Then we will tie them together.

The concept of a kingdom and knighthood may be a bit difficult for us 21st Century Americans to identify with and really understand because, as Americans, we are not accustomed to this kind of rule. As a matter of fact, over two hundred years ago this country rebelled against a king, King George of England, and the American Revolution in 1776 resulted. We established a government known as a Republic, which has an elected president as its leader. The president's son does not inherit the presidency.

Given all this as an historical backdrop, let's move ahead now and try to understand our role and obligation in the Family of God as sons and daughters of the supreme King, the King of Kings, the Creator of Heaven and Earth, and most importantly, sons and daughters of Our Father who is in Heaven.

New Testament Background

We've taken a very brief look at the Old Testament and have seen the background to understanding what a kingdom is. Now let's turn to the New Testament and see how Jesus uses this knowledge of how God's family is set up and how He applies it to Himself, and to you and me.

JESUS AS KING,
THE CATHOLIC CHURCH AS THE NEW ISRAEL,
THE KINGDOM AND FAMILY OF GOD

The King: In the New Testament, we read how Jesus was ultimately crucified for claiming to be a king. When Jesus was questioned by Pilate, He made it clear that He was a king and that He had a kingdom. But He also clearly stated that His kingdom was not of this world (John 18: 33–38). So Jesus is a king, and He has a kingdom. But remember what we said earlier, that a king received his throne from his father. So, if Jesus received His throne from His Father, then His Father must also have been a king. Look at 1 Samuel 8: 4–7. You will notice that God was the King over Israel, and when the people of Israel rebelled against Him, He allowed them to have an earthly king to govern them. This is made clear when God tells Samuel, *"… for they have not rejected you, but they have rejected me from being king over them."* But it would be God who appoints the king; only He keeps the people of Israel as His own (1 Sam 9:16-17). So Jesus being the Son of God, the King of Israel, truly was the heir to the throne and was definitely a king. He reinforces His kingship when He states *"all things have been delivered to Me by My Father"* (Matt 11:27). So we see here that Jesus is a true King who rules the Kingdom of God, His Father.

The Kingdom: Now the second thing we must look at in our attempt to understand the idea of the Kingdom of God is the term "kingdom" itself. We saw in the Old Testament that the nation of Israel was God's kingdom on earth. But in the New Testament, Jesus said that His kingdom is not of this world (John 18:33–38). Jesus' kingdom is of heaven and He came to establish His kingdom here on earth and expand God's kingdom to all the nations of the earth, not just the nation of Israel (Rev 7:9). Jesus began His public ministry by proclaiming that *"the Kingdom of Heaven is at hand"* (Matt 4:17). Later, we see that the people entered this kingdom by means of baptism with *"water and the spirit"* (John 3:3–6).

Notice also what St. Basil the Great said in this regard. In his Treatise on the Holy Spirit, St. Basil the Great (329–379 A.D.) explains:

> *"Through the Spirit, we became citizens of heaven, we are admitted to the company of the angels, we enter into eternal happiness, and abide in God."*

So now we have another brick in the building of our understanding of the family of God and how the Sacrament of Confirmation fits into this picture. The Kingdom of Heaven, established by Jesus, is a kingdom composed of those who believe and are baptized with water and Spirit, i.e. Baptism and Confirmation.

The Queen Mother: Let us now direct our attention to the queen mother seated at the right hand of the King of Israel. We have already determined that Jesus is a King. So we must now focus on His mother, Mary, and see if she is in fact the Queen Mother over the Kingdom of Heaven, like the queen mother over the Kingdom of Israel. In John's Gospel, we see that when Jesus is on the cross, His mother and the disciple whom Jesus loved were there with Him. Jesus then said to His mother, *"Woman, behold your son,"* and to the disciple He said, *"Behold your mother"* (John 19:25–27). We have to ask a question here. Who was the disciple that Jesus loved and gave His mother to? The answer is that Jesus loves all His disciples. The ones who followed Him then, and the ones who would follow Him in the future. So these words of Jesus have a symbolic meaning as well as a literal one. Jesus is giving His mother to all those who follow Him, to all those who are part of His Kingdom where He reigns as King and His mother as Queen Mother. We can see this better if we look again at the Book of Revelation and John's vision on the Lord's Day. John sees a woman clothed with the sun and the moon under her feet and on her head a crown of twelve stars (Rev 12:1). Notice this woman is wearing a crown like a queen.

Then she gives birth to a son, a male child, destined to rule all the nations with an iron rod. Her child is then caught up to God and His throne (Rev 12:5). After this, John sees a war break out in heaven and the dragon is thrown to earth and pursues the woman but to no avail. Then, because the dragon could not get to the woman, he went off to wage war against the rest of her offspring.

Now who is the woman? Who gave birth to a male child who would rule all nations and was taken up to God and His throne? The answer is Mary. But the real understanding of Mary as the queen mother over this kingdom, and we as her children, is at the end of Chapter 12. *"Then the dragon was angry with the woman and went off to make war on the rest of her offspring, on those who keep the commandments of God and bear testimony to Jesus"* (Rev 12:17). So Jesus' mother is, in fact, the Queen Mother over His kingdom and Mother to all those *"who keep the commandments of God and bear testimony to Jesus"* (Rev 12:17).

Structure and Cabinet Members: Let's look now at the hierarchy of the kingdom. We have already determined that Jesus is the king of the kingdom. But as we saw in the Old Testament, there were other offices instituted by the king so that in his absence, someone in the kingdom or palace would have his authority. It is important that we look at Isaiah 22:15-22 before we go any further, because we will see this imagery when we look at the hierarchy that Jesus established in the Kingdom of God on Earth, the Church.

The Prime Minister: In Isaiah, we see that there is a wicked steward or *master of the palace* named Shebna, who is a disgrace to his master's house. God is saying that He will throw Shebna out of his office and replace him with Eliakim, who is the servant of God. God also says that He will place the keys to the kingdom of David on the shoulders of Eliakim, so that when he opens, no one will shut, and when he shuts, no one will open.

Keep this Old Testament passage in mind. Now look at Matthew 16:17, 19. Here we see Jesus instituting this same office of *prime minister* or *master of the palace* and entrusting it to one of His disciples as He prepares to depart. When speaking to His disciples, Jesus asks, *"Who do men say that the son of man is?"* After a series of answers, Peter speaks up and says that Jesus is the Messiah, the Son of the Living God. Jesus then changes Peter's name from Simon to Peter, which means rock, and says, *"...and on this rock I will build my church and the powers of death shall not prevail against it. I will give to you the keys of the Kingdom of Heaven, and whatever you bind on earth shall be bound in heaven; and whatever you loose on earth shall be loosed in heaven"* (Matt 16:17–19).   Here, Jesus instituted the office of Steward of the Kingdom with the keys of His Kingdom being placed in that office. This parallels the Old Testament passage from Isaiah perfectly.

Cabinet Members: Just as there were various offices in the Old Testament that assisted the master of the palace or the prime minister in the governance of the kingdom, so too did Jesus do the same throughout His ministry with the twelve apostles. While Peter is the head of the "college of apostles," Jesus shared His authority with the other apostles as well. He sent them out to preach and heal in His name and on the night He rose from the dead, He appeared to the apostles and said, *"If you forgive the sins of any, they are forgiven; if you retain the sins of any, they are retained"* (John 20:22). Here, Jesus shares with His apostles His authority to forgive sins.

Jesus also makes these offices clear when He states to the apostles, *"As my Father appointed a kingdom for me, so do I appoint for you that you may eat and drink at my table in my kingdom, and sit on thrones judging the twelve tribes of Israel"* (Luke 22: 29-30).

With the institution of the office of the papacy and the college of the apostles, Jesus established His kingdom here on earth, and that Kingdom is the Catholic Church.

Knights or Soldiers of the Kingdom: But who will defend and spread this Kingdom of God on Earth? Does this duty belong only to the pope and the bishops and priests? No.

Just as we saw that the nation of Israel in Old Testament times had warriors or soldiers who were duty-bound to defend and spread the kingdom, so too is each one of us called to be a "knight of the kingdom," a "soldier of Christ," whose duty it is to defend and spread the Kingdom of God on Earth. And it is the Sacrament of Confirmation that empowers us to do so.

SOLDIERS OF THE KINGDOM

The Church's understanding of herself as the Kingdom of God on Earth and her subsequent need for soldierly defense and protection has been clear throughout the centuries. This quote from Hugh of St. Victor (1140) from his work, *On the Sacraments of the Christian Faith*, captures the imagery well:

"For the Incarnate Word is our king, Who came into this world to war with the devil; and all the saints who were before His coming are soldiers as it were, going before their king, and those who have come after and will come, even to the end of the world, are soldiers following their king. And the king Himself is in the midst of His army and proceeds protected and surrounded on all sides by His columns. And although in a multitude as vast as this, the kind of arms differ in the sacraments and observance of the peoples preceding and following, yet all are really serving the one king and following the one banner; all are pursuing the one enemy and are being crowned by the one victory."

This idea of warfare is again expressed in the General Catechetical Directory, 11 April 1971, in Section 57:

"Since the life of Christians, which on earth is warfare, is liable to temptations and sins, the way of the Sacrament of Penance is open for them, so that they may obtain pardon from the merciful God and reconcile themselves with the Church" (General Catechetical Directory, 11 April 1971).

Christians are called to warfare, but it is a spiritual warfare, a warfare in which we can be wounded by sin, and this sin could eventually lead to our spiritual death as well (mortal sin). We also see that the Sacrament of Penance is the spiritual Red Cross and "medic" on the scene of the battle to heal our wounds and revitalize us when we are mortally wounded.

The next question that a good soldier needs to ask is, *"Who is the enemy that I will be going into battle against?"* St. Cyril of Jerusalem gives us the answer to this question.

In 350 A.D., St. Cyril of Jerusalem gave a series of lectures during Easter week to the newly initiated members of the Church. He spoke on the liturgical ceremonies of the three sacraments which they had received during the Easter Vigil. When speaking about Confirmation, he stated:

"Just as Christ, after His baptism and the coming upon Him of the Holy Spirit went forth and defeated the adversary, so also with you. After holy Baptism and the Mystical Chrism, having put on the full suit of armor of the Holy Spirit, you are to withstand the power of the adversary, and defeat him, saying, 'I am able to do all things in Christ, Who strengthens me.'"

Here, St. Cyril of Jerusalem tells us two things about our battle. First, he identifies the enemy. Our enemy is the same one whom Jesus, our King, defeated in the desert—Satan. Secondly, the saint reminds us that before any soldier can go into battle, he must first be fully trained, fully armed, fully strengthened, and fully protected. It is the Sacrament of Confirmation that effects this. By virtue of the sacrament, we put on the full suit of armor that is the Holy Spirit Himself. Hence, Confirmation strenthens us as a *knight in shining armor,* a soldier resplendent with, empowered by, and strengthened through the glory of God. And this grace makes us strong to defend our own soul.

But, the sacramental graces of Confirmation make us strong to defend more as well. Recall that another duty of the knight is to be *devoted to the service of a lady as her attendant or champion.* Who is the lady of the Catholic soldier? It is the Church, the Bride of Christ, for whom Jesus will come back at the end of time.

The Book of Revelation makes this clear in Chapter 21, Verse 2:

"And I saw the holy city, new Jerusalem, coming down out of heaven from God, prepared as a bride adorned for her husband; and I heard a loud voice from the throne saying, 'Behold, the dwelling of God is with men. He will dwell with them, and they shall be his people, and God himself will be with them...'" The Book of Revelation goes on to say, *"'Come, I will show you the Bride, the wife of the Lamb.' And in the Spirit he carried me away to a great, high mountain, and showed me the holy city Jerusalem coming down out of heaven from God, having the glory of God, its radiance like a most rare jewel, like a jasper, clear as crystal"* (Rev. 21:9-11).

God is among us. His body, blood, soul, and divinity is in the tabernacle of every Catholic Church in the world. The Catholic Church is the New Jerusalem that came down from heaven. She is the Bride of the Lamb, Jesus Christ. And we are all called to be Her "knight in shining armor," Her champion and Her defender until the Lamb comes for His bride. What an awesome task at hand! A task for which we have been equipped, empowered, and commissioned through the Sacrament of Confirmation. But our King has given us all that we need. Recall St. Cyril of Jerusalem on Confirmation: *"I am able to do all things in Him, who strengthens me."* (Philippians 4:13)

We see this strengthening taking place when the Apostles received the Holy Spirit on Pentecost. They were all together in the upper room in fear of the Jews, and obeying Jesus' instructions to wait for the promise of the Father before going to Jerusalem. When the Holy Spirit descended upon the apostles they went out in power to preach and teach and those who accepted their message were baptized, and about three thousand persons were added that day (John 20:19, Acts 1:2-47).

This is the strength given to each one of us through the Sacrament of Confirmation. And this understanding has been consistent throughout Church history. This is what we will discover in the next section.

Biblical Origins and Implicit References

From Sacred Scripture to the present time, Church teaching is consistent regarding the Sacrament of Confirmation. A clear catena (chain of teaching), it instructs us that its fundamental efficacy is to strengthen in us the graces we received at Baptism. This is done through the power of the Holy Spirit filling us anew.

Early Church (1ˢᵗ–4ᵗʰ Centuries)

We can see from Sacred Scripture that the apostles understood the Sacrament of Confirmation was distinct from the Sacrament of Baptism, but yet connected in a special way to strengthen the one being confirmed in his baptismal graces. Just as they had been strengthened by the outpouring of the Holy Spirit in the Upper Room, so too did the apostles impart the Holy Spirit. This was done by the *Laying on of Hands.*

This is clearly seen in the Book of Acts. St. Luke writes:

"Now when the apostles at Jerusalem heard that Samaria had received the word of God, they sent to them Peter and John, who came down and prayed for them that they might receive the Holy Spirit; for it had not yet fallen on any of them, but they had only been baptized in the name of the Lord Jesus.

They then laid their hands on them and they received the Holy Spirit" (Acts 8:14-17 RSV).

"And Paul said, John baptized with the baptism of repentance, telling the people to believe in the one who was to come after him, that is Jesus. On hearing this, they were baptized in the name of the Lord Jesus. And when Paul had laid his hands upon them, the Holy Spirit came on them..." (Acts 19:4-6 RSV).

In 2 Corinthians, St. Paul writes:

"But it is God who establishes us with you in Christ, and has commissioned us; He has put His seal upon us and given us His Spirit in our hearts as a guarantee" (2 Cor 1:21 RSV).

The understanding that the Holy Spirit is imparted through the Laying on of Hands continues to develop. In the 2nd Century, Tertullian highlights this understanding as well as the distinction between the Sacrament of Baptism and the Sacrament of Confirmation. Consider this quote:

"The flesh is washed that the soul may be made stainless. The flesh is anointed that the soul may be consecrated. The flesh is sealed that the soul may be fortified. The flesh is overshadowed by the imposition of hands that the soul may be illuminated by the Spirit."

In yet another place, Tertullian also tells how the devil imitates the rites of Christian initiation, sprinkles some and signs them as his soldiers on the forehead (De resurr. canis n.8 Catholic Encyclopedia, 1908, pg. 218).

Writing a little more than one hundred years later, St. Cyril of Jerusalem instructed the newly initiated members of the Church about the liturgical ceremonies of the three sacraments which they had received at the Easter Vigil. The following three quotes refer specifically to the Sacrament of Confirmation. The first quote explains the efficacious relationship between the anointing with sacred oils and the imparting of the Holy Spirit. The second quote speaks to the efficacy of the sacrament in preparing the one confirmed for spiritual battle. And the third quote reminds us that through the Sacrament of Confirmation the confirmed are sealed by the Holy Spirit and strengthened as true soldiers of Christ.

"But beware of supposing that this is ordinary ointment. For just as the Bread of the Eucharist after the invocation of the Holy Spirit is simple bread no longer, but the Body of Christ, so also this holy ointment is no longer plain ointment, nor, so to speak, common, after the invocation. Rather, it is the gracious gift of Christ; and it is made fit for the imparting of His Godhead by the coming of the Holy Spirit. This ointment is symbolically applied to your forehead and to your other senses; and while your body is anointed with the visible ointment, your soul is sanctified by the holy and life-creating Spirit."

"Just as Christ, after His baptism and the coming upon Him of the Holy Spirit, went forth and defeated the adversary, so also with you. After Holy Baptism and the Mystical Chrism, having put on the full suit of armor of the Holy Spirit, you are to withstand the power of the adversary, and defeat him saying, 'I am able to do all things in Christ, who strengthens me.'"

"Forget not the Holy Spirit," he says to the catechumens, *"at the moment of your enlightenment; He is ready to mark your soul with His seal.... He will give you the heavenly and divine seal which makes the devil tremble; He will arm you for the fight; He will give you strength"* (Seventeenth catechesis on the Holy Spirit. Catholic Encyclopedia, 1908).

St. Ephream Syrus (circa 373 A.D.) also speaks to the sealing character of the Sacrament of Confirmation and the sacrament's efficacy in "suiting up" the confirmed for the battle:

"Chrism and Baptism; oil also for a most sweet unguent, wherewith they who already have been initiated by Baptism are sealed, and put on the armor of the Holy Spirit" (Serm 27, Catholic Encyclopedia, 1908, p. 218).

Middle Ages (5th –16th Century)

Continuing into and through the Early Middle Ages and to their end, the Church's teaching on the Sacrament of

Confirmation remains consistent. Theologians and saints of this period remind the people of God that they have been sealed and strengthened by the Holy Spirit, they have been equipped for spiritual battle, and through Jesus Christ they have been made victorious.

Consider this quote, for example, originally attributed to Eusebius of Emesa, but now known to come from a bishop of Southern Gaul in the 5th Century. It is part of a lengthy homily for *Whitsunday,* an ancient name for Pentecost Sunday:

"The Holy Ghost who comes down with a life-giving descent upon the waters of baptism, in the font bestows beauty unto innocence, in confirmation grants an increase unto grace. Because we have to walk during our whole life in the midst of invisible enemies and dangers, we are in baptism regenerated unto life, after baptism we are confirmed for the battle; in baptism we are cleansed, after baptism we are strengthened … confirmation arms and furnishes weapons to those who are reserved for the wrestlings and contests of this world" (Bib. Max., SS. PP., VI, p. 649).

St. Isidore of Seville, who lived from 560–636 A.D., had this to say about the Sacrament of Confirmation and its efficacy:

"… for as in baptism remission of sins is given, so by anointing [unctio] the sanctification of the Spirit is conferred. The

imposition of the hands takes place in order that the Holy Spirit, being called by the blessing, may be invited [per benedictionem advocatus invitetur Spiritus Sanctus]; for after the bodies have been cleansed and blessed, then does the Paraclete willingly come down from the Father" (Etym., VI, c.xix in P.L., LXXXII, col. 256)

The English priest and historian, John Lingard (1771–1851) writes this about St. Cuthbert, a bishop of the 7th Century:

"The confirmation of the newly baptized, was made an important part of the bishop's duty. We repeatedly read of journeys undertaken by St. Cuthbert chiefly with this object. Children were brought to him for confirmation from the secluded parts of the country; and he ministered to those who had been recently born again in Christ the grace of the Holy Spirit by the imposition of hands, 'placing his hand on the head of each, and anointing them with the chrism [sacred oil] which he had blessed'" (Anglo-Saxon Church, I, p.296).

Recall the earlier quote by Hugh of St. Victor. Writing during the Middle Ages, he makes it vividly clear that Christ is Our King, that He leads His soldiers in a war against the devil, and that the sacraments are efficacious in uniting us with Jesus Christ, the One King, through Whom the victory is won. Here is that quote again:

"For the Incarnate Word is our king, who came into this world to war with the devil; and all the saints who were before His

coming are soldiers as it were, going before their king, and those who have come after and will come, even to the end of the world, are soldiers following their king. And the king himself is in the midst of His army and proceeds protected and surrounded on all sides by His columns. And although in a multitude as vast as this the kind of arms differ in the sacraments and observance of the peoples preceding and following, yet all are really serving the one king and following the one banner; all are pursuing the one enemy and are being crowned by the one victory." (On the Sacraments of the Christian Faith, 1140 A.D.)

St. Thomas Aquinas, writing in Summa Contra Gentiles in the latter part of the 13th Century, explains that the Sacrament of Confirmation begins the strengthening process but does not complete it. He also explains how the sacrament makes the confirmed *a front-line fighter for the faith of Christ.* Again, this quote by St. Thomas Aquinas underscores the consistent teaching of the Church regarding Confirmation:

"The perfection of spiritual strength consists properly on a man's daring to confess the faith of Christ in the presence of anyone at all, and in a man's being not withdrawn therefrom either by confusion or by terror, for strength drives out inordinate terror. Therefore, the sacrament by which spiritual strength is conferred on the one born again makes him in some sense a front-line fighter for the faith of Christ. And because fighters under a prince carry his insignia, they who receive the Sacrament of Confirmation are signed with the Sign of the Cross by which He fought and conquered. This sign they receive on the forehead as a sign

that without a blush they publicly confess the faith of Christ."
Modern Times (16ᵗʰ Century–Present)

Following the Protestant Revolt in the 16ᵗʰ Century, the Church assembled an official Catechism called *The Roman Catechism or Catechism of the Council of Trent.* This Catechism was ordered by the Council of Trent (1545–1563), edited under St. Charles Borromeo, and published by decree of Pope St. Pius V. In 1905, Pope Pius X prescribed it to be used by all priests in instructing the faithful. Addressing the Sacrament of Confirmation, the Catechism of the Council of Trent states the clear and consistent teaching of the Church. It says this:

"If ever there was a time demanding the diligence of pastors in explaining the Sacrament of Confirmation, in these days certainly it requires special attention, when there are found in the holy Church of God many by whom this sacrament is altogether omitted; while very few seek to obtain from it the fruit of divine grace which they should derive from its participation." It goes on to say, *"Their instructions should so treat the nature, power, and dignity of this sacrament, that the faithful may understand not only that it is not to be neglected, but that it is to be received with the greatest piety and devotion."*

The Catechism of the Council of Trent states this about the name of the Sacrament and its strengthening power:

"...this sacrament is called by the Church 'Confirmation' because, if there is no obstacle to the efficacy of the Sacrament,

baptized persons, when anointed with the sacred chrism by the Bishop, with the accompanying solemn words..., becomes stronger with the strength of a new power, and thus begins to be a perfect soldier of Christ."

Writing in his ecyclical, *Mystici Corporis* (1943), Pope Pius XII had this to say about the Sacrament of Confirmation. Again, notice its consistency with prior Church teaching and the call of the soldier (knight) to defend his Lady:

"By the chrism of Confirmation, the faithful are given added strength to protect and defend the Church, their Mother, and the faith She has given them" (Mystici Corporis, 1943).

As we have discovered, there are many aspects to the Sacrament of Confirmation and the Church has held to them throughout the centuries. These aspects of the Sacrament are beautifully expressed in the *Documents of the Second Vatican Council* (196 –1965). The documents, *Lumen Gentium* and *Apostolicam Actuositatem,* reminds that through Confirmation the confirmed are strengthened to spread and defend the faith by word and deed. By fulfilling this obligation, they are a true witness of Christ:

"By the Sacrament of Confirmation, they [the baptized faithful] are more fully bound to the Church and the Holy Spirit endows them with special strength, so that they are more strictly obliged to spread and defend the faith, both by word and deed, as true witnesses of Christ" (Lumen Gentium n.11).

"The laity derive the duty and the right to the apostolate from their very union with Christ as head. Incorporated into the Mystical Body of Christ by baptism, and strengthened by the power of the Holy Spirit in Confirmation, they are assigned to the apostolate by the Lord Himself. They are consecrated to form a kingdom of priests and a holy people, so that by all their actions they may offer spiritual sacrifices and bear witness to Christ throughout the world" (Apostolicam Actuositatem, 1965).

Following the Second Vatican Council, Pope Paul VI reiterated the clear teaching of the Church about the Sacrament of Confirmation. In the following two quotes, the Holy Father talks about the imparting of the Holy Spirit, the obligation and duty that the Sacrament of Confirmation bestows on the one confirmed, the strengthening power of the sacrament, and the call of the confirmed to witness to Christ:

"Through the Sacrament of Confirmation, those who have been born anew in baptism receive the ineffable (indescribable) gift, the Holy Spirit Himself, by which 'they are endowed with special strength' and by the character of this sacrament 'are bound more perfectly to the Church' and 'are more strictly obliged, as true witnesses of Christ, to spread and defend the faith by word and deed...'" (Apostolic Constitution Divinae Consortium Naturae, 1971)

"In the Sacrament of Confirmation the Apostles and the Bish-

ops, *who are their successors, hand on to the baptized the special gift of the Holy Spirit, promised by Christ the Lord and poured out upon the Apostles at Pentecost. Thus the initiation in the Christian life is completed so that believers are strengthened by power from heaven, made true witnesses of Christ in word and deed, and bound more closely to the Church"* (S.C.D.W., Decree Peculiare Spiritus Sancti donum, 1971).

These same realities of the Sacrament are also expressed in *Canon Law*, the body of laws and regulations adopted by ecclesiastical authority to govern the Church and its members. Canon Law 879 states:

"The Sacrament of Confirmation impresses a character and by it the baptized, continuing on the path of Christian initiation, are enriched by the gift of the Holy Spirit and bound more perfectly to the Church; it strengthens them and obliges them more firmly to be witnesses to Christ by word and deed and to spread and defend the faith."

Like his predecessors, Pope John Paul II upheld, encouraged, and proclaimed the Church's clear and consistent teaching on the Sacrament of Confirmation. In April, 1992, he used his weekly catechesis as a forum to instruct the faithful about the sacrament's strengthening character:

"The grace conferred by the Sacrament of Confirmation is more specifically a gift of strength. This gift corresponds to the need for greater zeal in facing the 'spiritual battle' of faith and charity in order to resist temptation and give the wit-

ness of Christian word and deed to the world with courage, fervor and perseverance. This zeal is conferred by the Holy Spirit" (L'osservatore Romano, 8 Apr 92. Summa Theol. III, q.72, a.5).

During the pontificate of Pope John Paul II, the Catholic Church released the *Catechism of the Catholic Church.* Published in 1994, it was the first work of its kind since the *Catechism of the Council of Trent* issued almost 500 years earlier.

Again, the *Catechism of the Catholic Church* unequivocally states the consistent teaching on the Sacrament of Confirmation. Consider the following paragraphs from the *Catechism:*

#1285   *"Baptism, the Eucharist, and the sacrament of Confirmation together constitute the "sacraments of Christian initiation," whose unity must be safeguarded. It must be explained to the faithful that the reception of the sacrament of Confirmation is necessary for the completion of baptismal grace. For "by the sacrament of Confirmation, [the baptized] are more perfectly bound to the Church and are enriched with a special strength of the Holy Spirit. Hence they are, as true witnesses of Christ, more strictly obliged to spread and defend the faith by word and deed."*

#1302   *"It is evident from its celebration that the effect of the sacrament of Confirmation is the full outpouring of the Holy Spirit as once granted to the apostles on the day of Pentecost.*

#1303   *From this fact, Confirmation brings an increase and deepening of baptismal grace:*

—it roots us more deeply in the divine filiation which makes us cry, "Abba! Father!"

—it unites us more firmly to Christ;

—it increases the gifts of the Holy Spirit in us;

—it renders our bond with the Church more perfect;

—it gives us a special strength of the Holy Spirit to spread and defend the faith by word and action as true witnesses of Christ, to confess the name of Christ boldly, and never to be ashamed of the Cross:

Recall then that you have received the spiritual seal, the spirit of wisdom and understanding, the spirit of right judgment and courage, the spirit of knowledge and reverence, the spirit of holy fear in God's presence. Guard what you have received. God the Father has marked you with his sign; Christ the Lord has confirmed you and has placed his pledge, the Spirit, in your hearts."

PART II

As we have seen, the Sacrament of Confirmation is a strengthening sacrament. It imbues the soul with a new character that increases the efficacy of the graces received at baptism, and enables the confirmed to wage a holy war against the powers and principalities that are the enemies of the soul and the enemies of the Church. In Part II, we will explore common misconceptions about the Sacrament of Confirmation, and we will approach some practical considerations regarding it.

Misconceptions

The Sacrament of Confirmation is both underrated and poorly understood. Because of this, many people today have misconceptions about the sacrament.

As a Confirmation Coordinator and religious educator, I read and heard many references to the Sacrament of Confirmation that deviated from Church teaching or, by over-emphasizing and exaggerating certain aspects of it, distorted its true efficacy. Following are some examples of what is commonly misperceived about the sacrament.

It is the *Sacrament of Maturity*: This term suggests that a person being confirmed had reached an age where they have now become a mature Christian in their faith and, as a result of the successful completion of the Confirmation program, are now mature enough to receive the Sacrament of Confirmation and become full members of the Church.

It is the *Sacrament of Adulthood in the Church* or *The Christian Bar-Mitzvah*: Similar to the above term, this understanding of the sacrament means the confirmed is now ready to assume positions in the Church like lector, usher, and other ministry positions. One national Catholic publication compared the Sacrament of Confirmation to a Jewish bar mitzvah, where the one confirmed passes into adulthood and Confirmation is the ceremony that celebrates this.

It is the *Sacrament of Choice*: This term means the person being confirmed makes an adult choice to be Catholic and "confirms" that choice through reception of the Sacrament of Confirmation. This misconception is very common among both students and parents.

These terms beg the point of the Sacrament of Confirmation, and distort its true meaning and value. Additionally, they deny the literal meaning of the word *"confirmation"* which means *"strengthening."*

The Sacrament of Confirmation is the *Sacrament of Strengthening*. This name underscores that the gifts we received at Baptism are strengthened by the Holy Spirit. The Holy Spirit does the *"confirming"* or *"strengthening."* We do not do it for ourselves by selection or choice of the sacrament.

What The Sacrament Is Not

The previous list of misconceptions spells out for us what the Sacrament of Confirmation is not. Let's unpack each of these with a little more detail. First, Confirmation is not the *Sacrament of Christian Maturity.* This misconception implies that the one being confirmed has already "arrived" when, in fact, the one being confirmed is only now receiving the strength to embark upon his journey toward spiritual maturity—a journey that can last a lifetime and even go beyond.

This is what St. Thomas Aquinas alludes to in *Summa Contra Gentiles.* Following is the quote again. Read it and notice that it is in cooperation with the strength the Holy Spirit imparts at Confirmation that a person can become spiritually mature:

The perfection of spiritual strength consists properly on a man's daring to confess the faith of Christ in the presence of anyone at all, and in a man's being not withdrawn therefrom either by confusion or by terror, for strength drives out inordinate terror. Therefore, the sacrament by which spiritual strength is conferred on the one born again makes him in some sense a front-line fighter for the faith of Christ.

This selection suggests that while spiritual strength is conferred upon the person through the Sacrament, it must be engaged to become mature. It is the lived experience of the grace that leads to the *perfection of spiritual strength*. This is the consistent understanding and teaching of the Church. Therefore, Confirmation is not an acknowledgment of the spiritual maturity a person has attained, but rather a strengthening point from which spiritual maturity (perfection) can develop.

Another misconception, as we have seen, is the notion that the Sacrament of Confirmation is the *Sacrament of Adulthood in the Church* or the equivalent of the Jewish Bar Mitzvah (*Bat Mitzvah*, for girls). This is problematic because on the one hand it equates spiritual growth with the reality of physical development, and on the other, compares it to a "rite of passage" completely different from the *strengthening* reality of the Sacrament of Confirmation. Regarding the former, there is no direct correlation between physical age and spiritual maturity. Some of the greatest saints were spiritually mature at a very young age, while many people who are well on in years are near infantile in their spiritual understanding. As we discussed above, grace is given but grace must be acted upon in order to be fully realized. We must correspond with the grace.

To properly understand the difference between Jewish Bar Mitzvah and Confirmation, it is important to understand what the Jewish Bar Mitzvah is all about.

Literally, the term *Bar Mitzvah* means "son of the commandment" and it technically refers to a child's "coming of age" from the standpoint of religious obligation. In the Jewish religion, although children are encouraged to observe the commandments, they are not obligated to do so until the age of 13 for boys and 12 for girls. At these ages, boys are said to become *bar mitzvah* and girls are *bat mitzva* (pronounced *"bas mitzvah")*—obligated. This is a rite of passage that takes place without any formal act, celebration, or ceremony. It happens by attaining a certain age, and at that age rights and obligations are now incumbent upon the child. Stated simply it means a child is now held responsible for his actions. In this sense, *bar (bat) mitzvah*, more closely parallels the Catholic understanding of the "age of discretion" rather than Confirmation.

In addition to obligating the child to the ordinance of the commandments, bar mitzvah also gives them the right to take part in leading religious services, to count the number of people present to perform certain parts of religious services (*minyan*), to form binding contracts, to testify before religious courts, and to marry. The *bar mitzvah* ceremony and celebration is a relatively new feature and is entirely unnecessary to the reality taking place. Nothing is conferred via the ceremony or the celebration, and the ceremony and the celebration are completely ancillary to the reality.

Like the Sacrament of Confirmation, however, the bar mitzvah is not the final goal of religious education. It is not a graduation ceremony. The call to continue to study the *Torah* remains an obligation throughout the child's life. In some synagogues, the rabbi even has the child sign an agreement to continue his education after bar mitzvah.

The final misconception is that Confirmation is *The Sacrament of Choice* wherein the confirmand chooses to be Catholic and *confirms* his decision. Again, the confirmand does not do the *confirming*. It is the Holy Spirit who confirms (strengthens) the confirmand by means of the Sacrament of Confirmation.

As for making the choice to be Catholic, the parents made that choice when the child was baptized. This is in full accord with their God-given authority to properly rear their child in the knowledge of God. God has entrusted parents with the souls of their children to lead them to Him.

This responsibility cannot be taken lightly. It requires parents to make certain that, in addition to the Sacrament of Baptism, their children receive the other two Sacraments of Initiation: Confirmation and Eucharist. Speaking to this responsibility, the Sacred Congregation for Divine Worship, in its Rite of Confirmation states:

"The initiation of children into the sacramental life is ordinarily the responsibility and concern of Christian parents. They are to form and gradually increase a spirit of faith in the children and, at times with the help of catechism classes, prepare them for the faithful reception of the Sacraments of Confirmation and Eucharist. The role of the parents is also expressed by their active participation in the celebration of the sacraments" (Rite of Confirmation, DOL 2513).

So to say that the Sacrament of Confirmation is making a mature decision and choosing to be Catholic is again misstating and clouding the true meaning of the sacrament.

What Confirmation Is

So what then **IS** Confirmation if it **IS NOT** *The Sacrament of Christian Maturity, The Sacrament of Adulthood in the Church* or *The Christian Bar Mitzvah*, or *The Sacrament of Choice*? To answer, recall again the words of Pope Paul VI regarding the Sacrament and its efficacy:

"Through the Sacrament of Confirmation, those who have been born anew in baptism receive the ineffable (indescribable) gift, the Holy Spirit Himself, by which 'they are endowed with special strength' and by the character of this sacrament 'are bound more perfectly to the Church' and 'are more strictly obliged, as true witnesses of Christ, to spread and defend the faith by word and deed...'" (Apostolic Constitution Divinae Consortium Naturae, 1971).

Here, the Holy Father reminds us that the Sacrament of Confirmation confers upon the confirmand a *special strength* through the gift of the Holy Spirit Himself; that the confirmand becomes bound—more perfectly bound—to the Church; and that the confirmand now is *strictly obliged* to *spread and defend the faith.*

Writing in the 13th Century, St. Thomas Aquinas also gives us keen insight into the Sacrament of Confirmation as well as its interrelatedness with the other sacraments of initiation and the sacraments of healing. To do so, he compares spiritual life to bodily life. He writes:

"*[1] However, since the spiritual remedies of salvation have been given to men under sensible signs, it was suitable also to distinguish the remedies provided for the spiritual life after the likeness of bodily life.*

"*[2] Now, in bodily life we find a twofold order: for some propagate and order the bodily life in others; and some are propagated and ordered in the bodily life.*

"*[3] Now, in a bodily and natural life three things are necessary of themselves, and a fourth incidentally. For first, by generation or birth a thing must receive life; second, by growth it must arrive at its due size and strength; third, both for the preservation of life acquired by generation and for growth, nourishment is necessary. And these are of themselves necessities for natural life, because without these bodily life cannot be perfected; wherefore, one assigns to the vegetative soul which is the principle of life the three natural powers: that of generation, that of growth, and that of nourishment. But, since there can be an impediment to natural life from which the living thing grows weak, a fourth thing is incidentally necessary; this is the healing of the sick living thing.*

"*[4] Thus, then, in the spiritual life, also, the first thing is spiritual generation: by baptism; the second is spiritual growth leading to perfect strength: by the sacrament of confirmation; the third is spiritual nourishment: by the sacrament of the*

Eucharist. A fourth remains, which is the spiritual healing; it takes place either in the soul alone through the sacrament of penance; or from the soul flows to the body when this is timely, through extreme unction. These, therefore, bear on those who are propagated and preserved in the spiritual life" (Summa Contra Gentiles, vol.4).

St. Thomas' analogy is a good one. First, he helps us to see that just as a person is born into this life as an infant in the human family, Baptism is the rebirth into the spiritual life as an infant in God's family.

Second, St. Thomas points out that, just as the physical body grows until it reaches *"its due size and strength"*, Confirmation is what enables *"spiritual growth leading to perfect strength."* Notice that he says *"leading to perfect strength."* He doesn't say that Confirmation is the declaration of strength already attained. Confirmation makes it possible for the reborn, infant soul to begin its growth processes toward becoming a mature Christian.

Third, St. Thomas shows that the Eucharist is necessary for spiritual nourishment just as nourishment is necessary for *the preservation of life* and *for growth.*

This point is also made in the Catechism of the Catholic Church: *"The sacraments of Christian initiation—Baptism, Confirmation, and the Eucharist—lay the foundations of every Christian life. 'The sharing in the divine nature given to men through the grace of Christ bears a certain likeness to the origin, development, and nourishing of natural life. The faithful are born anew by Baptism, strengthened by the sacrament of Confirmation, and receive in the Eucharist the food of eternal life. By means of these sacraments of Christian initiation, they thus receive in increasing measure the treasures of the divine life and advance toward the perfection of charity."* (Catechism of the Catholic Church #1212)

In summary then, the Church's teaching on the interrelatedness of all three sacraments of Christian initiation and their necessity for spiritual maturity is consistent. Baptism "births" us into the family of God. Confirmation strengthens us in our new life and equips us to live it. Eucharist, our spiritual food, provides us sustenance. It nourishes us and helps us to grow in our life in God.

Imagine, if you will, what would happen if you were to withhold the necessities of natural life—conception and birth, nourishment, growth and strength—from the human body. Life would not exist at all or once it was begun it could not be sustained. Life would wither, degenerate, and die.

So, too, with spiritual life. Without Baptism, there is no spiritual birth. The life of the soul doesn't even begin. Without Confirmation, there is no spiritual growth or maturation. Life is stunted and handicapped. Without Eucharist, there is no spiritual nourishment. Life cannot be sustained. Thus, all three sacraments of Christian initiation are intrinsic to and necessary for attaining spiritual maturity.

But, does the interrelatedness of these three sacraments and their importance for the spiritual life tell us something more as well? Could it suggest that we reconsider the age at which the Sacraments of Initiation be received? Let's take a look at the much debated question regarding the age at which the Sacrament of Confirmation should be conferred.

The Age of Confirmation

In the United States, the age at which the Sacrament of Confirmation should be conferred is hotly debated among religious educators, catechists, and the ecclesial establishment.

The first thing we need to do is to look at the age which the Church, in her wisdom, has set for those receiving the Sacrament of Confirmation. To find this, we will first look at Canon Law, Section 891, the Rite of Confirmation, and finally the Rite of Christian Initiation of Adults (RCIA).

Canon Law, Section 891 says this about the age at which confirmation should be administered:

The Sacrament of Confirmation is to be conferred on the faithful at about the age of discretion unless the conference of bishops determines another age or there is danger of death or in the judgment of the minister a grave cause urges otherwise.

While this is helpful, it leads to yet another question: What is the age of discretion? The Rite of Confirmation gives us the answer. It says, *"With regard to children in the Latin Church the administration of Confirmation is generally delayed until about the seventh year."*

This is helpful information. The quote from The Rite of Confirmation seems to indicate that *"the age of discretion"* is around the age of seven. If so, then it seems to suggest it is the mind of the Church to confirm children at a much younger age than the current trend of adolescence. Is this the case? The Rite of Christian Initiation of Adults says *"yes."* Section 14 says, *"The priest who baptizes an adult or a child of catechetical age should, when the Bishop is absent, also confer confirmation..."* This tells us that parents and their children of catechetical age receive all three sacraments of Christian Initiation at once—Baptism, Confirmation, and Eucharist.

Why do you suppose the Church, in her wisdom, would set the norm for receiving The Sacrament of Confirmation at this particular age? Remember what it is that Confirmation strengthens us against. As you recall from Part I, the General Catechetical Directory, 11 April 1971, states the following:

"Since the life of Christians, which on earth is warfare, is liable to temptations and sins, the way of the Sacrament of Penance is open for them, so that they may obtain pardon from the merciful God and reconcile themselves with the Church".

This statement tells us that our life here on earth is a spiritual warfare. And in this warfare we are liable and wounded by sin. But at what age are we capable and liable for committing sin? The answer is *the age of discretion* or *about the seventh year*. How appropriate it is that the Church has provided a means for our young people to counter the seductive forces of this world through reception of this most glorious Sacrament of Confirmation. It provides the spiritual strengthening needed to counter the world, the flesh, and the devil at the very age at which they become accountable for sin—the age of 7.

God has not left us orphaned. He has not sent us up a creek without a paddle. In the spiritual battle of the Christian life God has made it possible for the baptized to be spiritually strengthened to fight the good fight. Without this strength, children at this age cannot fight off the attacks of sin effectively.

Let's use the analogy of a new military recruit. Once accepted into the service the recruit enters into a training process— boot camp or basic training as it is called. In boot camp, the recruit begins to learn the art of soldiering. He receives his uniform, his battle gear, his weaponry. He uses them to become skilled and to attain battle knowledge. During this time, the new soldier also works hard to become physically conditioned and strong. He builds his endurance.

And so it is with the Sacrament of Confirmation. Confirmation is the spiritual means God provides to become strengthened for the warfare of the Christian life. In this sacrament, the newly confirmed *Soldier of Christ* receives his battle gear and weaponry: the helmet of salvation, the breastplate of righteousness, the belt of truth, the shield of faith, the sword of the Spirit which is the word of God, and the boots of zeal to spread the Gospel (Ephesians 6:13-17).

But, like the new military recruit, the newly confirmed is not yet a seasoned soldier. He has not developed or matured his skills nor has he grown strong through the test of combat. However, like the military recruit, the newly confirmed has received the tools and the strength he needs to develop his full potential as a Soldier for Christ.

The Sacrament of Confirmation is critical for victory in the spiritual battle. It seems to make little sense, then, to delay conferring it much beyond the age of discretion at which time a child becomes capable of sin and culpable for it.

It makes better sense, and seems to be spiritually wiser and pastorally more responsible, to administer the Sacrament of Confirmation to every baptized Catholic at or about the age of seven in accord with the mind of the Church. That being said, it might even be better to consider conferring the sacrament at the time of infant baptism as is done in the Eastern Church. To confer the sacrament at a younger age, however, would require a restructuring of many current parish religious education programs.

Religious Education:
A New Look

While religious education and instruction are essential for sacrament preparation, they are also necessary to prepare a person for eternal life. Recall the analogy St. Thomas Aquinas provided in the *Summa Contra Gentiles* where he compares the physical and spiritual development of the person. Let's apply this same analogy to the area of a person's secular and spiritual education.

When a person is of school age (in our society today, it is about the age of 5) he begins a secular education process, learning the very basics of what he will one day need in the future to be a productive, healthy, positive member of society. This process is well-rounded and encompassing.

He will learn how to read, write, work out mathematical problems, study and memorize events in history so he can learn from the past. This education will form him and help provide him with a lens to see and understand the world and it will lay the foundation for him to achieve his potential.

High School education builds on these years. The student has matured in knowledge, in experience, in mental ability. He begins to form his own identity as a member of society and to see himself as contributing to a good greater than his own needs and wants. He is maturing and is making his way from childhood to adulthood.

Upon completion of high school, a person begins to narrow his academic endeavors to those areas of study that will best serve his personal needs and the needs of society at large. He seeks proficiency in his given field of interest through continuing education and a continued personal drive to be the very best he can be. Hopefully, the student's education becomes a life-long pursuit that leads to accomplishment and the attainment of his goals.

Now let's take what we have said about the secular educational development of a person and apply it to religious education. When a person is of catechetical age (in the Catholic Church it is about the age of 5) he begins a religious education process to learn the basics of living a just and holy life and how to attain salvation. He learns about the Ten Commandments, the beatitudes, morality, love, kindness, forgiveness. He studies and memorizes events in salvation history so as to make a personal connection with that history and call it his own. It is to be a well-rounded religious education that enables the person to live his faith in the world today and to achieve eternal life tomorrow.

Adolescence should bring a greater knowledge of the Faith as well as a deepening appreciation of it. Studies advance and so does understanding. A connection between religious teaching and daily life begins to develop for the student. Faith begins to inform social behavior and general interaction with others.

As the student enters young adulthood, he begins to isolate a field or vocation that would best serve the family of God and personally aid him in answering God's call for his life. He pursues his call throughout adulthood continuing to grow and develop in his vocation: religious life, the priesthood, marriage or the celibate life. This continuing spiritual formation happens through individual study, prayer, adult education classes, and seminars, but specifically through each local parish.

Take a look at the following diagram. Notice the duration of time between "Birth" and "Death/Judgment." Then look at the duration of time between "Death/Judgment" and "Eternity". This timeline portrays temporal life and its relationship to the Four Last Things (Death, Judgment, Heaven, Hell). How, then, can we develop our religious education program with this ultimate reality in mind? The next section will give us one alternative.

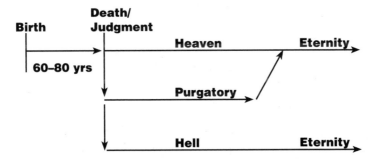

A Plan for Restructuring

Every parish should provide a catechetical program to teach the faith from K–12. It should continue with an optional Adult Education program following 12th grade for those who desire to advance their spiritual knowledge and for those who have completed RCIA and are seeking to continue their education of the faith.

For all of the reasons outlined prior, the Sacrament of Confirmation should be conferred at about the age of discretion. Structurally, the change would require very little adjustment to the existing program. However, it would be desirable to draw a connection between Baptism and Confirmation for the student when the Sacrament of Baptism is being taught, usually in the first grade.

In this construct, the Sacrament of Confirmation would be received prior to First Holy Communion. This restores the order of the sacraments of Christian Initiation culminating with reception of the Eucharist through which the fully initiated member of the Church joins our Lord in the Eucharistic Banquet, the wedding feast of the Lamb.

The higher grade levels would require a more involved restructuring. In addition to the catechetical program for these age groups, the students' social development and needs must also be addressed. This can be accomplished by combining Youth Group activities with classroom instruction specifically focused on apologetics and evangelization.

Adolescence and young adulthood are years of questioning, seeking, and exploring. "Who am I?" "Why am I?" and "What is my purpose in life?" are common questions, and many teens struggle in their attempts to answer them.

In addition, they want to know how their faith impacts their daily lives and why what they believe should be believed. "Prove it!" is an oft heard cry and it is the job of the catechist and instructor to do just that. We must respond to the command given to us by St. Peter to *"make a defense to anyone who calls you to account for the hope that is within you..."* (1 Peter 3:15).

Giving a reasonable explanation and defense to our young people about the Catholic faith is eminently necessary for the successful passing on of the faith in a world saturated with an anti-Gospel message. For this reason, developing a high school religious education program that pivots on the Church's art of apologetics makes good and reasonable sense.

Fr. William Most wrote a book for teens titled *Catholic Apologetics Today* published by TAN Books and Publishers. The following is an extensive quote from that book explaining exactly what we are trying to deal with here:

"A strange phenomenon appears in most young people sometime near the end of high school. It starts then, and lasts varying lengths of time—sometimes for years—and is of varying severity.

"The symptoms? The young person finds his formerly solid religious beliefs beginning to wobble. He is no longer sure of them; and he is hesitant to ask an older person, for he is definitely inclined not to trust the opinions of any older person. So he is forced to be miserable all by himself, unless of course he talks to others of the same age and finds them in the same quandary, but equally without any way to get out.

"We said the length of time this trouble lasts is varying; some never fully emerge from it. That brings us to see the first of the reasons for the problem. When we were children, we simply believed what older people told us. Really, that is all that could be done at an early age. But then as we grow up, we begin to want to know for ourselves, to be able to give a reason for what we believe.

"This process is not only quite normal; it can even be a good thing, provided that it is carried all the way to its conclusion. If not, a person may lack stability indefinitely, perhaps for the rest of his life. This process is, then, the normal changeover from the child to the adult pattern of beliefs. It is proper, because adults should not act like children and should be able to give a reason for their beliefs.

"No one can be quite comfortable between the shore of childhood belief and the shore of solidly grounded adult faith. For, there is neither fish nor fowl. He lacks both kinds of security and so he flounders. Eventually he may just give up trying, but yet never achieve the solidity he reasonably wants. Worse, if some great test of faith comes, he may not have the solid basis on which to endure.

"Obviously, the rational thing for a young, even older person to do in such a quandary is to ask for help from those who are able to give it. Sadly, this is not so often done. First, the young persons are disinclined to think older persons could possibly know anything; second, many older persons never completed the rational process themselves, and are really in no position to help.

"There is a second very potent reason for this 'at-sea' condition. Young people are apt to have their somatic resonance in a state of flux. Somatic resonance is a common term in psychology. It is not hard to understand. A major psychologist of our times, T. V. Moore, told in his last book of a case he met when he was a practicing psychiatrist in Washington, D.C. A patient came in for help who suffered from manic-depressive psychosis. He told Dr. Moore he was losing his faith. Moore reported that the man really was not losing his faith; instead, the process of the disease was interfering with his somatic resonance to faith.

"Here is the way it works. We are, of course, made up of body and soul, matter and spirit. These elements are so closely joined as to add up to one person. As a result of that union if we

have a condition on either side, body or soul, then for smooth running (not for mere survival of the condition) we ought to have a parallel condition on the other side. That parallel is called a resonance. When the resonance is on the side of the body—the more common combination—then it is called somatic resonance, from a Greek word meaning "bodily."

"So, then, faith is obviously on the side of the spirit. But faith needs—not for mere survival, but for normal function—a resonance on the bodily side. The process (probably bad biochemistry) of the disease in Moore's patient interfered with the somatic resonance to faith. [The result was that faith was not rejected, but neither could it function normally.] Hence, the poor man thought he was losing his faith.

"Now, young people can have a parallel problem. They enter a time of life when there are great bodily changes in the glandular system, especially at the start of sexual functioning. They have not yet had time to learn to live with these changes, to come to terms with them. As a result, their somatic resonance to many things is in a state of flux, so that faith lacks its normal resonance. No wonder faith tends to wobble, to seem to have no foundation.

"Obviously, if a young person could only realize what is going on inside him and see that he is being hit by a dramatic changing process, he would be very relieved. We do not say he would quickly find everything easy. But he could step outside himself and see himself objectively. Then at least he would not be so mystified by what he cannot help feeling.

"The two conditions we have just explained are clearly part of the process of growing up. As such, they have always affected people, not just in our day. But today, young and old alike are affected by still a third influence: the immense upheaval in the Church and the many claims that everything has changed. It is no wonder many are uncomfortable with their Faith."

We see here how Fr. Most not only identifies what is going on with our young people, but also provides reinforcement for our suggestion above: give our students a reasonable defense and explanation of the faith, and focus the catechetical curriculum in the junior high and high school levels on Apologetics and Evangelization.

In summation, if the sacrament of Confirmation were placed at the age of discretion or before, it would allow the Holy Spirit and the Catechist to work together hand in hand; the Catechist, providing the knowledge and external intellectual stimulation; and the Holy Spirit, through the Sacrament of Confirmation, strengthening the seven gifts received at Baptism—Knowledge, Wisdom, Understanding, Right Judgment (or Council), Courage (or Fortitude), Reverent Love (or Piety), and Holy Fear (or Fear of the Lord), working from within the individual, assisting that person to understand and embrace the truths the catechist presents in the name of Jesus Christ.

What a combination this could be, but it must be done correctly. Our faith is a living, breathing faith. It cannot be reduced to a textbook, or a series of memorized questions and answers. These things are important, but our faith is far more than this. We are children of the Eternal and Almighty God Himself, and all that God has done in salvation history is our heritage and our history.

We are heirs of the Kingdom of Heaven and the creator of the Heavens and the Earth is none other than our Father! Isn't this enough to make us shout from the roof tops to anyone who will listen? Have we done our best to convey this to our youth of today? Let's enter back into partnership with the Holy Spirit in the religious education of our young people, and stop trying to do it all ourselves.

If Confirmation were received at or before the age of discretion, the Holy Spirit would not be left to work on His own as He is today. We are trying to teach our youth heavenly truths without the heavenly strengthening to understand these truths. We need to stop placing the cart before the horse. A child cannot walk until his leg muscles are first strong enough to support his weight. Let the Holy Spirit strengthen the individual in the Sacrament of Confirmation, and then watch the spiritual and catechetical formation bloom as he continues his walk on the road to our heavenly homeland.

Thomas K. Sullivan
Tom@CalledToKnighthood.com
www.calledtoknighthood.com

AUTHOR BIO

After a 12-year career serving in the United States Military, Tom Sullivan returned to the Catholic Faith at the age of 30 and found his true mission in life. Using the same determination, skills and abilities that made him a successful and highly decorated military leader, Tom has spent the past 18 years in Catholic evangelization, education and apologetics.

In 1992 following a disabling injury which brought his military career to an end, Tom began working with St. Joseph Communications in California. During this time, he developed evangelization and educational materials for both national and international audiences. Tom also conceived and developed the Scott and Kimberly Hahn Adult Education on Video program now in thousands of homes and parishes. Tom is a founding member of the National Catholic Family Conference held each year in California and was the 1996 recipient of the annual Fulton J. Sheen award for his work in evangelization.

In 2001, Tom joined the staff of Living His Life Abundantly® International, Inc. He serves as the Director of Information Technology and Network Administrator and Senior radio engineer. He has appeared on EWTN's "Life on the Rock" and "The Abundant Life" Television Programs as well as Women of Grace LIVE radio, Faith and Family Radio and Sieze the Day with Gus Lloyd on SIRIUS Satellite Radio.

In addition, Tom has extensive experience teaching youth confirmation preparation and parish adult education classes as well as speaking to both adults and teens on the many topics concerning the Catholic Faith.

He continues to spend much of his free time speaking to youth, adults, and catechists about the importance of Confirmation and its relationship to spiritual knighthood.

Tom has been married to his wife, Carol, since 1982. They are the parents of six children and the grandparents of eight grandchildren.